# JURASSIC EXPLORERS PRESENTS

# THE WORLD OF DINOSAURS

## FUN, PLAY & LEARN

### ACTIVITY BOOK

D1076132

## Contents

Little Brother BOOKS

Published 2022.

Little Brother Books Ltd, Ground Floor,
23 Southernhay East, Exeter, Devon EX1 1QL
books@littlebrotherbooks.co.uk | www.littlebrotherbooks.co.uk

Printed in the United Kingdom.

## SPOT IT!

Can you find the fossil hidden on this page?

# TIME CHALLENGE

Use a clock or a watch to time yourself.

This baby Iguanodon has lost its herd. How quickly can you lead it back to its family, avoiding the predators along the way?

**START**

Answers on page 48.

**FINISH**

# HOW LONG DID IT TAKE?

Less than a minute = colour the clock green.
1-2 minutes = colour the clock blue.
More than 2 minutes = colour the clock red.

# TYRANNOSAURUS

I was one of the **scariest** dinosaurs to ever walk the Earth!

**IT'S A FACT!**
I could swallow small dinosaurs whole.

**WOW!**
My deadly bite was three times as powerful as a lion's.

I walked on two legs.

## Fierce Facts

**NAME:** TYRANNOSAURUS (TYE-RAN-OH-SORE-US)  **MEANING:** TYRANT LIZARD  **FOOD:** MEAT  **SIZE:** 12M

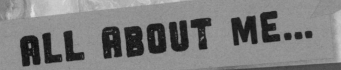

My huge brain was twice the size of other meat-eaters.

**DID YOU KNOW?**
I had a sharp sense of smell which I used to sniff out prey.

I had 60 sharp teeth that could bite through bone.

Scientists don't really know why my arms were so small.

## UP CLOSE

One of these close-ups doesn't belong to me. Can you spot the imposter?

A

B

C

D

# DINO CHANGES

There are **eight differences** between these two dinosaur pictures. Can you spot them all?

**a**

Colour a dinosaur footprint each time you spot a difference.

Answers on page 48.

# ALL ABOUT ME...

# SPINOSAURUS

You can recognise me by the **eye-catching sail** on my back.

## DINNERTIME

Which trail should I follow to find the fish?

A B C

**WOW!**
At 16m, I was the longest meat-eating dinosaur.

## Fierce Facts

**NAME:** SPINOSAURUS (SPINE-OH-SORE-US)  **MEANING:** THORN LIZARD  **FOOD:** MEAT AND FISH  **SIZE:** 16M

**DID YOU KNOW?** Scientists don't really know why I had a sail. It could have cooled me down or helped me to stay underwater.

My nostrils were high up so I could breathe underwater.

My bony sail was enormous.

My sharp teeth were like a crocodile's.

**IT'S A FACT!** I hunted for food on land and in the water.

I had webbed feet to help me walk in water.

9

# TERRIFYING T-REX

Use your favourite pens to colour the **dinosaur king.**

## SPOT IT!

Can you find this dinosaur egg?

# WHICH DINO ARE YOU?

Choose your favourite picture from each row to find out which dinosaur you're most like!

**A**  **B**  **C**  **D**

FOOD

PLACE

COLOUR

PLANT

ANIMAL

**Mostly As - Tyrannosaurus**

You are strong and brave, just like a Tyrannosaurus.

**Mostly Bs - Diplodocus**

You're a Diplodocus. You have lots of friends and are very kind.

**Mostly Cs - Spinosaurus**

You like to stand out from the crowd, just like a Spinosaurus.

**Mostly Ds - Stegosaurus**

You're a Stegosaurus. You like to chill out and are very thoughtful.

# TRICERATOPS

I was the **biggest** of all the horned dinosaurs.

My bulky body meant I couldn't walk very fast.

## LOTS OF LEAVES

Count how many leaves I have collected for my lunch.

**There are** [ ] **leaves.**

## Fierce Facts

**NAME:** TRICERATOPS (TRI-SERRA-TOPS)   **MEANING:** THREE-HORNED FACE   **FOOD:** PLANTS   **SIZE:** 9M

# EGG BOX DINO

This Triceratops is so **fun to make,** you'll want to create a whole dino family!

## YOU WILL NEED

Cardboard egg box

Paper cupcake case

Pipe cleaner

Paint          Googly eyes

Skewer

Paintbrush

Scissors     PVA glue

## HOW TO MAKE

**1**

Cut a section from the base of the egg box to make the dinosaur's head.

**2**

Paint the egg box section in your chosen colour and leave it to dry.

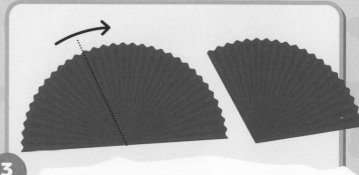

**3**

Fold the cupcake case in half and flatten it, then fold one side in to make a fan shape.

**4**

Glue the cupcake case to the egg box head.

**5**

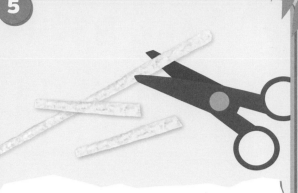

Cut three pieces from the pipe cleaner, each about 3cm long.

**6**

Use a skewer to carefully pierce three holes in the egg box head where the three horns will go.

**7**

Push a pipe cleaner piece through each hole and bend it back on the underside to hold it in place.

**8** Glue on some

# GOOGLY EYES

to finish your egg box Triceratops.

Adult guidance is needed for this activity.

You can make your dinosaur in any colour you like.

# VELOCIRAPTOR

I may have been small but I was *super speedy*.

My long tail helped me balance when I ran.

## EGG HUNT

Can you find five dinosaur eggs hidden on these pages? Tick a circle as you spot each one.

## WOW!

I was only the size of a large dog.

## Fierce Facts

**NAME:** VELOCIRAPTOR (VEL-OSS-EE-RAP-TOR)  **MEANING:** SPEED THIEF  **FOOD:** MEAT  **SIZE:** 2M

Answers on page 48.

# LEAFY LUNCH

**This Stegosaurus has a rumbling tummy!** Can you lead it to its favourite plants, completing the activities along the way?

Trace the trail with a pencil and complete the activities along the way.

**START**

**1** Colour the flying reptile.

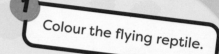

**2** Circle the biggest boulder.

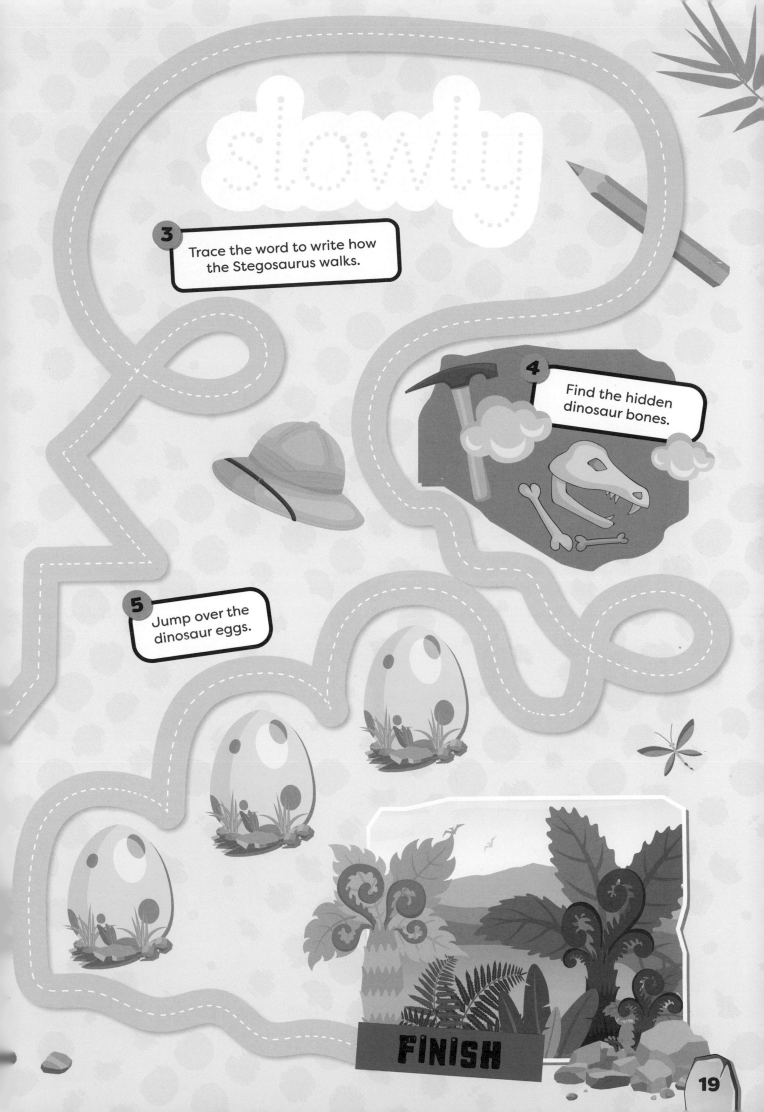

**slowly**

**3** Trace the word to write how the Stegosaurus walks.

**4** Find the hidden dinosaur bones.

**5** Jump over the dinosaur eggs.

**FINISH**

# ALL ABOUT ME...
# STEGOSAURUS

I lived in the USA **145 million years ago.**

## SHADOW MATCH

Which of these shadows belongs to me?

My spiked tail was a useful weapon against attackers.

A

B

C

I had an enormous body the size of an elephant's.

## Fierce Facts

**NAME:** STEGOSAURUS (STEG-OH-SORE-US)  **MEANING:** ROOF LIZARD  **FOOD:** PLANTS  **SIZE:** 9M

  Answers on page 48.

IT'S A FACT!
I had a tiny brain that was only the size of a walnut.

WOW!
My back plates may have flashed red to frighten away attackers.

I had two rows of bony back plates.

My beak-like mouth was super sharp.

DID YOU KNOW?
I didn't have any teeth. Instead I used my beak to nip low growing plants.

# WHO'S HIDING?

Can you work out which dinosaurs are **hidden** behind the trees? It's trickier than you think!

Answers on page 48.

Tick a circle as you spot each dinosaur, but be careful, only four of these dinosaurs are actually hiding – the other two are just there to trick you!

A  B  C  D  E  F

# ALL ABOUT ME...

# IGUANODON

I lived in **England, Belgium** and the **USA**.

## LEAFY LUNCH

Draw lines to match these leaves into pairs.

A

B

C

D

E

F

G

H

**IT'S A FACT!**
Two hundred years ago, I became the first ever plant-eating dinosaur to be identified by a scientist.

I could walk on either two or four legs.

## Fierce Facts

**NAME:** IGUANODON (IG-WHA-NOH-DON)  **MEANING:** IGUANA TOOTH  **FOOD:** PLANTS  **SIZE:** 9M

WOW!
I had really strong bones in my legs to support my heavy body.

DID YOU KNOW?
When I was first discovered, scientists thought my thumb spike was a head horn.

My grooved teeth were good at grinding plants.

I had a long tongue.

I used my large thumb spike to fend off attackers.

# PREHISTORIC PAL

Use these pages to **design** your very own dinosaur.
How it looks, what it eats and the skills it has are all up to you!

## DINOSAUR REPORT

NAME: _____ osaurus

AGE: _____ million years

### SIZE:

Tiny ○

Small ○

Medium ○

Big ○

Ginormous ○

### FOOD:

Meat ○

Plants ○

Fish ○

Berries ○

Insects ○

### FEATURES:

Sharp teeth ○

Long neck ○

Back plates ○

Horns ○

Tail spike ○

### SKILLS:

Speed ○

Strength ○

Fierce roar ○

Powerful bite ○

Sharp eyesight ○

**Draw your dino here.**

**Is your dinosaur's tail long or short?**

**What colour is your dinosaur?**

**Does your dinosaur walk on two legs or four?**

# ALL ABOUT ME...

# DIPLODOCUS

**I was one of the longest land creatures to ever live on Earth.**

My long tail had 80 backbones.

My strong back legs were longer than my front legs.

## PATTERN PUZZLE

What colour egg comes next in the sequence? Colour the last egg the right colour.

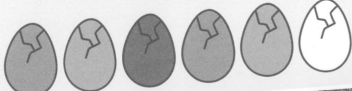

## Fierce Facts

**NAME:** DIPLODOCUS (DIP-LOW DOCK-US)  **MEANING:** DOUBLE BEAM  **FOOD:** PLANTS  **SIZE:** 27M

IT'S A FACT!
I was as long as
two buses.

WOW!
I used my tail
like a whip to scare
off attackers.
It made a loud
booming sound.

I used my long
neck to reach high
up plants.

DID YOU KNOW?
I swallowed stones
to help digest the food
in my stomach.

I had narrow,
pointy teeth.

# FOOTPRINT T-REX

Stomp like a dinosaur when you make this fun T-Rex picture using your own footprints!

Make sure you read page 32 before you cut out the page. If you don't want to cut up your book, use a piece of white A4 paper instead.

## YOU WILL NEED

Scissors

Glue

Green paint

Paintbrush

Googly eye

Marker pen

## HOW TO MAKE

**1** Ask an adult to cut out the page opposite.

**2** Paint the sole of one of your feet with green paint, then make a footprint on the page.

**3** Paint the sole of your other foot and add another footprint to the page, slightly overlapping the first.

**4** Once the paint has completely dried, used a black felt tip pen to draw teeth in your footprint dinosaur's mouth.

**5** Finally, glue on a googly eye and leave the glue to dry.

Cut out the page along this line.

Adult guidance is needed for this activity.

If you don't want to get messy, you can draw around your feet instead.

# ALL ABOUT ME...
# MICRORAPTOR

### I looked like a bird and was covered in feathers.

## ODD ONE OUT

Can you circle the picture that is different to the rest?

**A**

**B**

**C**

I had really sharp claws.

The fan of feathers on the end of my tail helped me balance in the air.

## Fierce Facts

**NAME:** MICRORAPTOR (MIKE-ROW-RAP-TOR) **MEANING:** SMALL THIEF **FOOD:** MEAT **SIZE:** 40CM

Answers on page 48.

33

# PARASAUROLOPHUS

**You can recognise me by my fancy head crest.**

I had an unusual shaped tail.

## BIG AND SMALL

Can you circle the biggest fossil and cross out the smallest?

A

B

C

I could stand on my back legs to reach high up leaves.

## Fierce Facts

**NAME:** PARASAUROLOPHUS (PA-RA-SAW-ROL-OFF-US)  **MEANING:** NEAR CRESTED LIZARD  **FOOD:** PLANTS  **SIZE:** 9M

# DINOSAUR FUNNIES!

These Jurassic jokes are **roar-some!**

**What does a Triceratops sit on?**

IT'S TRICERA-BOTTOM!

**How do you call a dinosaur to dinner?**

TEA, REX!

**Why shouldn't you ask a dinosaur to read you a story?**

BECAUSE THEIR TALES ARE SO LONG!

**Why does Diplodocus have such a long neck?**

BECAUSE ITS FEET STINK!

**What should you do when a dinosaur sneezes?**

GET OUT OF THE WAY!

**What do you call a dinosaur with no ears?**

ANYTHING YOU WANT, IT CAN'T HEAR YOU!

## RATE IT!

Colour a thumb to give each joke a thumbs up or a thumbs down.

36

# MEMORY GAME

Test your memory with this **fun game!** You can play on your own or with a friend.

## HOW TO PLAY

Now turn the page...

Look at the prehistoric pictures above for one minute, then turn to the next page and see how many you can remember.

# MEMORY GAME

Use this space to write or draw all the items you can remember from the previous page.

I REMEMBERED _____ OUT OF 10.

# FACT FINDER

Use the code to help you write an **awesome fact** about the fierce Coelophysis.

a   e   i   o   u

Coolophysos was ono f tho Earth's forst donosaors.

Write the fact here.

_____

_____

_____

_____

Answer on page 48.

# ALL ABOUT ME...

# ANKYLOSAURUS

**I moved slowly but I was incredibly tough.**

I used my tail club to attack predators.

My body was covered in studs to protect me like armour.

## FIND THE FOOTPRINTS

How many footprints can you find hidden on these pages?

I walked slowly because I was really heavy.

## Fierce Facts

**NAME:** ANKYLOSAURUS (AN-KIE-LOH-SORE-US) **MEANING:** STIFF LIZARD **FOOD:** PLANTS **SIZE:** 10M

# WHO AM I?

**A** Tyrannosaurus

**B** Ankylosaurus

**C** Parasaurolophus

Answers on page 48.

**Shhhhh,** there's a dinosaur asleep inside the cave. But who is it? Read the clues to work out the answer.

I can stand on two legs.

I am big.

I can make music with my head crest.

I have a pointed tail.

I eat plants.

Circle the dinosaur who's asleep in the cave.

**D**

Giganotosaurus

**E**

Triceratops

**F**

Microraptor

# OVIRAPTOR

**I was an unusual looking dinosaur with bird-like features.**

## COLOUR CODE

How many teeth did I have? Copy the letters below into the matching coloured circle to discover the answer.

E O N N

### IT'S A FACT!
I lived in the deserts of Mongolia and China.

### WOW!
I laid my eggs in a spiral shape.

## Fierce Facts

**NAME:** OVIRAPTOR (OH-VEE-RAP-TOR)  **MEANING:** EGG THIEF  **FOOD:** MEAT AND PLANTS  **SIZE:** 2.4M

45

# ALL ABOUT ME...

# GIGANOTOSAURUS

I was one of the **biggest** dinosaurs in the world.

## IT'S A FACT!
The only proof scientists have that I existed comes from one skeleton and a piece of jawbone.

## Fierce Facts

**NAME:** GIGANOTOSAURUS (GIG-AN-OH-TOE-SORE-US) **MEANING:** GIANT SOUTHERN LIZARD **FOOD:** MEAT **SIZE:** 12M

**WOW!**
My small brain was about the size of a cucumber.

**DID YOU KNOW?**
Some scientists believe I was bigger and heavier than the Tyrannosaurus.

I had a small brain for my size.

I had a sharp sense of smell.

I had three clawed fingers on each hand.

My blade-like teeth were good for slicing meat.

## QUESTION TIME

### I was a small dinosaur.
Circle the right answer.

**TRUE**     **FALSE**

47

# ANSWERS

## Pages 2-3

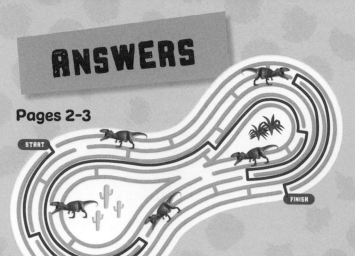

## Pages 4-5

The imposter is C.

## Pages 6-7

## Pages 8-9

Spinosaurus should follow trail B.

## Page 10

## Pages 12-13

There are 12 leaves.

## Pages 16-17

## Pages 20-21

Shadow C belongs to Stegosaurus.

## Pages 22-23

Only A, C, D and E are hiding.

## Pages 24-25

A and D, B and G, C and H, E and F.

## Pages 28-29

A blue egg comes next in the sequence.

## Pages 32-33

The odd one out is B.

## Pages 34-35

The biggest fossil is C, the smallest fossil is B.

## Page 39

Coelophysis was one of the Earth's first dinosaurs.

## Page 40-41

There are 5 hidden footprints.

## Pages 42-43

Parasaurolophus is sleeping in the cave.

## Pages 44-45

The answer is NONE.

## Pages 46-47

The answer is FALSE.